First Person

A ★ M ★ E ★ R ★ I ★ C ★ A

THE NATION DIVIDES

The Civil War (1820-1880)

Richard Steins

Twenty-First Century Books

**A Division of Henry Holt and Company
New York**

Twenty-First Century Books
A Division of Henry Holt and Company, Inc.
115 West 18th Street
New York, New York 10011

Henry Holt® and colophon are registered trademarks of Henry Holt
and Company, Inc.
Publishers since 1866

Published in Canada by Fitzhenry & Whiteside Ltd.
195 Allstate Parkway, Markham, Ontario L3R 4T8

Printed in the United States of America
All first editions are printed on acid-free paper ∞.

Created and produced in association with Blackbirch Graphics, Inc.

Library of Congress Cataloging-in-Publication Data

Steins, Richard.
    The nation divides: the Civil War, 1820–1880 / Richard Steins.— 1st
edition.
      p. cm. — (First person America)
    Includes bibliographical references and index.
    Summary: Primary source materials present different aspects of the
Civil War, including the debate over slavery, secession of the Confederate
States, the war itself, and life for the slaves after emancipation.
    ISBN 0-8050-2583-9 (alk. paper)
    1. Slavery—United States—History—Sources—Juvenile literature.
2. United States—History—1815–1865—Sources—Juvenile literature.
3. United States—History—Civil War, 1861–1865—Sources—Juvenile
literature. 4. Reconstruction—Sources—Juvenile literature. [1. Slavery—
History—Sources. 2. United States—History—1815–1865—Sources. 3.
United States—History—Civil War, 1861–1865—Sources. 4. Reconstruction—Sources.] I. Title. II. Series.
E441.S85 1993
973.5—dc20   93-24993
                                                         CIP
                                                            AC

CONTENTS

INTRODUCTION

The magnificent experiment in American democracy and self-government, which was born in revolution and enshrined in the noble ideals of the Declaration of Independence and the Constitution, was almost destroyed by slavery. Beginning in the 1820s, politics and society were dominated by this issue, which, in the South, was often thought of as a question of states' rights. Eventually, slavery brought the United States to the point of civil war in 1861.

Politicians as well as ordinary citizens argued about whether the institution of slavery was right or wrong, whether it should be outlawed or allowed to remain in existence, and whether it should be allowed to expand in the western territories. In the North, abolitionists—those who believed that slavery should be abolished totally and immediately—loudly proclaimed their points of view in newspapers and pamphlets from the 1830s on. Increasingly, the South felt under siege, believing that its distinct way of life—based on slavery—was now threatened by these Northerners.

In Washington, moderate politicians spent most of their energy trying to devise one compromise after another to prevent the nation from splitting apart. The Missouri Compromise of 1820 was supposed to limit slavery's expansion but at the same time preserve the balance of power between North and South in the federal government.

As the years passed, however, the voices of compromise were more and more drowned out as proslavery and antislavery positions hardened. Slavery—"the peculiar institution"—was driving the nation apart. By the 1850s, even the most skillful politicians seemed to have run out of compromises. In 1854, Senator Stephen A. Douglas of Illinois sponsored a bill, which, when enacted into law as the Kansas-Nebraska Act, repealed the Missouri Compromise and allowed slavery to expand in the western territories. To oppose this move, the antislavery forces joined together to form a new party—the Republican Party—and in 1860 it nominated a lawyer from Illinois named Abraham Lincoln for president.

Lincoln and Douglas had debated all the issues slavery raised when they ran for the Senate in Illinois in 1858. Douglas won then, but two years later, when the two men were pitted against each other in the presidential election, Lincoln was the victor.

Lincoln's election was the last straw for the South. Most Southern politicians believed that a Republican government under Lincoln would abolish slavery, even though Lincoln—who was personally opposed to slavery—believed that the government had no right to

The Battle of Corinth, Mississippi, was a major victory for the North during General Grant's 1862 campaign. The first engagement is shown here in this lithograph by Currier and Ives (*Library of Congress*).

tamper with it where it already existed. By early 1861, 11 Southern states had withdrawn from the Union. On April 12, 1861, the shooting began. For the next four years, America was immersed in a civil war that proved to be the bloodiest conflict in the nation's history.

The Civil War was a turning point for the United States. Under Lincoln's inspired leadership, the ideals of the Declaration of Independence—that all men are created equal—finally came to have meaning.

Although he did not live to see his triumphs fully realized, Lincoln witnessed the destruction of slavery and the reunification of the nation. However, the freed slaves would have to wait fully another hundred years before they achieved their rights. After the war, the North lost interest in African Americans and their problems, and the ex-slaves came once again under the power of their former white masters, who, over the years, took it upon themselves to deny their former slaves civil rights and liberties.

In this volume, we hear voices that tell us what a slave auction was like, and we hear the confession of a slave who tried to achieve freedom for his people by murdering any white person with whom he came into contact. We also hear the voices of the powerful and the oppressed—the eloquent pronouncements of a truly great president and the touching recollections of former slaves both before and after the Civil War. We hear the voices of those passionately defending slavery as a positive good and those speaking of it as the greatest evil on earth. And we see how this terrible and bloody war affected ordinary people—whether soldiers from the North or South or unknown slaves waiting silently on plantations in the South for the freedom they knew would surely come.

Abraham Lincoln's leadership during the Civil War helped to ensure victory for the North. In this famous photograph by Alexander Gardner, Lincoln (center, with top hat) inspects the headquarters of the Union Army at Antietam, October 1, 1862 (*National Archives*).

CHAPTER 1

SLAVERY: "THE PECULIAR INSTITUTION"

Buying and Selling Slaves

Though it is commonly referred to by historians as the "peculiar institution," slavery was not peculiar to the United States or to the nineteenth century. It has been in existence throughout history and has affected people in almost every culture.

Slavery was introduced into what is now the United States in 1619, when a Dutch merchant brought about 20 Africans to Jamestown, Virginia, and sold them to colonists. For many years, slavery was a part of life for the entire country. For a variety of reasons, however, it began to disappear in the North. Northerners had small farms and were shopkeepers and traders. There was no economic reason to buy and maintain large numbers of slaves. As small industries began to grow in the North in the early 1800s, mechanics rather than slaves were needed.

A slave trader inspects the hold of the slave ship *Gloria*, where newly captured men were packed together for their voyage to North America (*Library of Congress*).

The situation, however, was different in the South. Slavery was beneficial to the way of life there—it was an integral part of the economy and social structure. Because it was so entrenched, slavery remained an institution in that part of the country until it was abolished in 1865 by the Thirteenth Amendment to the U.S. Constitution.

To Southern plantation owners, slaves were property, in the same category as a chair, a horse, or a house. In the eyes of the law, slaves had no rights, despite the fact that they were highly valuable to their masters. Although the conditions under which slaves lived and worked were harsh—long hours in the field, poor food and living quarters—it was in the interest of the slave owner to make sure that the slaves did not get sick. If illness swept the slave quarters, a plantation owner's source of income could be lost, which would very likely bring about economic ruin.

The conditions under which slaves lived varied from plantation to plantation. In many cases, slaves were able to create a sense of community and protect themselves from the degrading and inhuman aspects of a system that gave them absolutely no rights.

Slaves were expensive. A healthy young man in the middle of the nineteenth century could cost as much as $3,000, which at that time was an enormous amount of money. Since slaves were property, they were traded as property. Although a slave owner could buy a slave from another person, one of the main ways of purchasing slaves was at auction. The slaves for sale would be displayed in front of a crowd of buyers, where they were examined closely to determine the state of their health. One of the greatest tragedies of the auction system was that it tore families apart. A buyer might well choose to purchase a man, but not his wife or child. Throughout the long years of slavery, there were countless numbers of people who were separated forever from their loved ones.

The moving passage that follows is an account by a former slave, Josiah Henson, of a slave auction held in about 1820.

People, Bought and Sold

My brothers and sisters were bid off first, and one by one, while my mother, paralyzed by grief, held me by the hand. Her turn came, and she was bought by Isaac Riley of Montgomery county. Then I was offered to the assembled purchasers. My mother, half distracted with the thought of parting forever from all her children, pushed through the crowd, while the bidding for me was going on, to the spot where Riley was standing. She fell at his feet, and clung to his knees, entreating him in tones that mother could only command, to buy her baby as well as herself, and spare to her one, at least, of her little ones. Will it, can it be believed that this man, thus appealed to, was capable not merely of turning a deaf ear to her supplication, but of disengaging himself from her with such violent blows and kicks, as to reduce her to the necessity of creeping out of his reach, and mingling the groan of bodily suffering with the sob of a breaking heart? As she crawled away from the brutal man I heard her sob out, "Oh, Lord Jesus, how long, how long shall I suffer this way!" I must have been then between five and six years old. I seem to see and hear my poor weeping mother now. This was one of my earliest observations of men, an experience which I only shared with thousands of my race.

From: *Truth Stranger Than Fiction, Father Henson's Story of His Own Life* by Josiah Henson (Boston: J. P. Jewitt & Co., 1858).

The Hope of Freedom

Over the long centuries of their enslavement, African Americans tried to maintain their own communities and family ties, despite the terrible conditions under which they lived. By the middle of the 1800s, many Southern states had passed laws making it a crime to teach slaves to read or write. An educated slave was considered a danger, a possible leader who might cause other slaves to rebel against their white masters. In addition to the many other restrictions that were placed on them, slaves were prohibited from getting married in Christian wedding ceremonies.

Over the years, however, many slaves were taught to read and write by their owners, and many also took on some form of their masters' religious faith. Slave culture had a deeply spiritual quality to it, which was often expressed in a yearning to be free some day. This sad, yet faithful, spirit is most visible in slave songs that have been passed down through the generations. These songs, most often patterned after the church spiritual, or hymn, were sung to provide strength and hope for a future that seemed bleak and hopeless. The words of the song on the next page make reference to the biblical story of Daniel and his deliverance from the lions. If Daniel could be saved from the lion's den, "why not every man"?

Didn't My Lord Deliver Daniel

Didn't my Lord deliver Daniel,
   deliver Daniel, deliver Daniel,
Didn't my Lord deliver Daniel,
An' why not every man.

He delivered Daniel from the lion's den,
Jonah from the belly of the whale,
An' the Hebrew chillun from the fiery furnace,
An' why not every man.

Didn't my Lord deliver Daniel,
   deliver Daniel, deliver Daniel,
Didn't my Lord deliver Daniel,
An' why not every man.

The moon run down in a purple stream,
The sun forbear to shine,
An' every star disappear,
King Jesus shall-a be mine.

The win' blows eas' an' the win' blows wes',
It blows like the judge-a-ment day,
An' ev'ry po' soul that never did pray'll
Be glad to pray that day.

Didn't my Lord deliver Daniel,
   deliver Daniel, deliver Daniel,
Didn't my Lord deliver Daniel,
An' why not every man.

From: *Afro-American History: Primary Sources*, Thomas R. Frazier and John M. Blum, eds. (New York: Harcourt Brace Jovanovich, 1970). Reprinted by permission.

Nat Turner led a slave revolt that strengthened the South's resolve to stop slavery reform. After his capture, Turner was tried and hanged along with 16 others (*North Wind Picture Archives*).

Slave Rebellion

Nat Turner was an African-American slave and also a skilled carpenter and a preacher. He was born in Southampton County, Virginia, on October 2, 1800. As a child he was deeply religious and very quickly learned to read. Turner believed that he was chosen by God to lead the slaves to freedom, and on August 21, 1831, he led a revolt with a band that grew to about 70 followers.

In just a few days, Turner and his group went from plantation to plantation in the county and murdered at least 57 white people, sparing neither women nor children. The revolt was eventually crushed, and 13 slaves and 3 free African Americans were quickly hanged. Turner was tried and sentenced to death. Shortly before his execution, on November 11, 1831, he was interviewed by Thomas R. Gray, who published Turner's remarks in a book called *The Confessions of Nat Turner* in 1832.

Turner's rebellion was one of the bloodiest slave uprisings in the South. It led to the passing of even more laws forbidding slaves to learn to read and to assemble in large groups. It also brought an end to all slavery-reform movements in the South.

In the following passages, Turner describes to Gray his early sense of uniqueness and the opening hours of his revolt.

Nat Turner's Insurrection

You have asked me to give a history of the motives which induced me to undertake the late insurrection, as you call it. To do so I must go back to the days of my infancy, and even before I was born. I was thirty-one years of age the second of October last, and born the property of Benjamin Turner, of this county. In my childhood a circumstance occurred which made an indelible impression on my mind, and laid the groundwork of that enthusiasm which has terminated so fatally to many both white and black, and for which I am about to atone at the gallows. It is here necessary to relate this circumstance—trifling as it may seem, it was the commencement of that belief which has grown with time, and even now, sir, in this dungeon, helpless and forsaken as I am, I cannot divest myself of. Being at play with other children when three or four years old, I was telling them something, which my mother overhearing, said it had happened before I was born. I stuck to my story, however, and related some things which went in her opinion to confirm it. Others being called on were greatly astonished, knowing that these things had happened, and caused them to say in my hearing, I surely would be a prophet, as the Lord had shown me things that had happened before my birth. And my father and mother strengthened me in this my first impression, saying in my presence, I was intended for some great purpose, which they had always thought from certain marks on my head and breast.

My grandmother, who was very religious, and to whom I was much attached—my master, who belonged to the church, and other religious persons who visited the house, and whom I often saw at

prayers, noticing the singularity of my manners, I suppose, and my uncommon intelligence for a child, remarked I had too much sense to be raised—and if I was, I would never be of any service to any one— as a slave.... As I was praying one day at my plough, the spirit spoke to me, saying "Seek ye the kingdom of Heaven and all things shall be added unto you."
Question—What do you mean by the Spirit?
Answer—The Spirit that spoke to the prophets in former days—and I was greatly astonished, and for two years prayed continually, whenever my duty would permit—and then again I had the same revelation, which fully confirmed me in the impression that I was ordained for some great purpose in the hands of the Almighty.... And as it had been said of me in my childhood by those whom I had been taught to pray, both white and black, and in whom I had the greatest confidence, that I had too much sense to be raised, and if I was I would never be of any use to anyone as a slave.

...And by signs in the heavens that it would make known to me when I should commence the great work—and until the first sign appeared, I should conceal it from the knowledge of men—and on the appearance of the sign (the eclipse of the sun last February), I should rise and prepare myself, and slay my enemies with their own weapons. And immediately on the sign appearing in the heavens, the seal was removed from my lips, and I communicated the great work laid out for me to do, to four in whom I had the greatest confidence (Henry, Hark, Nelson, and Sam).

From: *The Confessions of Nat Turner, Leader of the Late Insurrection in Southampton, Virginia, as Fully and Voluntarily Made to Thomas R. Gray, 1832* by Thomas R. Gray (Richmond, Virginia: 1832).

Plantation Overseers

The plantation overseer was the man hired by the owner to supervise slaves as they worked in the fields. An overseer was both a manager and a watchdog. He had to make sure that the slaves worked hard, but he also kept his eye open for any threats or rebellious behavior on the part of the slaves.

Plantation overseers and owners worked together at slave auctions, looking for the strongest and healthiest people to buy (*North Wind Picture Archives*).

The selection printed here is from an 1837 journal called the *Farmers' Register*. The writer points out that overseers must be honest and firm individuals but not petty tyrants. He also holds common mistaken ideas about African Americans at the time—that they cannot learn anything but can only imitate their superiors, that they are naturally prone to temptations such as stealing, and that they cannot tell the difference between right and wrong.

These views were commonly used to justify the existence of slavery. Because African Americans were believed to be inferior to whites, they needed the protection and discipline that slavery offered.

Throughout the history of slavery in America, there were all different kinds of overseers. Some of them were indeed cruel and vengeful, while others understood that gentleness would serve the interests of the plantation owner much more than harshness.

Advice from an Overseer

When negroes are accustomed to an overseer, and you dispense with the services of one, they *must* be exposed to a great deal of temptation, far more than they can resist. And education has not taught them the difference between right and wrong; at any rate, their ideas on the subject must be confused. What they learn of the moral code, is gathered from observation, and the example of others, their superiors. How can any person, who has no overseer, be at all hours with the negroes, when he is delivering his grain for example? Let him turn his back, and a cunning fellow will help himself to a bushel of corn or wheat, and he will never be informed upon by his fellow laborers, though ever so honest; for an informer, in their eyes, is held in greater detestation than the most notorious thief.

I admit that many overseers are vain, weak tyrants, "dressed in a little brief authority," but probably a larger proportion of farmers of Virginia are indifferent cultivators of the soil. I regard an overseer as an indispensable agent, whose first qualities should be honesty and firmness, united with forbearance and good temper.... A written agreement should be drawn up between the employer and the employed, to be signed by both, setting forth the terms, and mentioning the most important requisitions, which will occur to every one. An overseer's wages should always be paid in money; for if you give him a part of the crops, your land will be worked to death, and never have a dozen loads of manure spread upon it. In addition to this, your views and his will frequently come into collision.

From: *The Farmer's Register* (September 1837).

CHAPTER 2

DRIFTING TOWARD WAR

Views on Slavery

In the 1830s, in the wake of Nat Turner's rebellion, the national debate over slavery—and states' rights—intensified. On the side of the abolitionists, one of the more influential and vocal leaders was Theodore Dwight Weld, a Connecticut-born minister. Weld and his wife, Angelina Grimké, a rebellious daughter of a South Carolina plantation owner who was active in the antislavery movement, anonymously published a book called *American Slavery as It Is* in 1839. This book, together with Harriet Beecher Stowe's novel, *Uncle Tom's Cabin*, did more than any other publications to heighten the awareness of Americans of the cruelty and injustice of slavery. In the passages that follow, Weld recounts the recollections of a Mr. Caulkins, who lived many years in the South and witnessed the brutal effects of slavery.

Harriet Beecher Stowe's novel, *Uncle Tom's Cabin*, was one of the most influential books ever written about slavery (*National Portrait Gallery*).

Theodore Dwight Weld Against Slavery

I feel it my duty to tell some things that I know about slavery, in order, if possible, to awaken more feeling at the North in behalf of the slave. The treatment of the slaves on the plantations where I had the greatest opportunity of getting knowledge, *was not so bad* as that on some neighboring estates, where the owners were noted for their cruelty. There were, however, other estates in the vicinity, where the treatment was better; the slaves were better clothed and fed, were not worked so hard, and more attention was paid to their quarters.

The scenes that I have witnessed are enough to harrow up the soul; but could the slave be permitted to tell the story of his sufferings, which no white man, not linked with slavery, *is allowed to know*, the land would vomit out the horrible system, slaveholders and all, if they would not unclinch their grasp upon their defenceless victims....

It is customary for plantation owners to let the hogs run in the woods. On one occasion a slave caught a pig...which he carried to his quarters. The overseer, getting information of the fact, went to the field where he was at work, and ordered him to come to him. The slave at once suspected it was something about the pig, and fearing punishment, dropped his hoe and ran for the woods. He had got but a few rods, when the overseer raised his gun, loaded with duck shot, and brought him down. It is a common practice for overseers to go into the field armed with a gun or pistols, and sometimes both. He was taken up by the slaves and carried to the plantation hospital, and the physician sent for. A physician was employed by the year to take care of the sick or wounded slaves. In about six weeks this slave got better, and was able to come out of the hospital. He came to the mill where I was at work, and asked me to examine his body, which I did, and counted twenty-six duck shot still remaining in his flesh, though the doctor had removed a number while he was laid up.

From: *American Slavery as It Is: Testimony of a Thousand Witnesses* by Theodore Dwight Weld (New York: American Anti-Slavery Society, 1839).

The supporters of slavery were not without their champions. George Fitzhugh, a Virginia lawyer, was passionate in his defense of slavery as a positive thing for African Americans. His book *Sociology for the South*, a selection from which is given here, was published in 1854. Until the Nat Turner revolt, many Southerners had regarded slavery as a necessary evil. After the rebellion, however, more and more Southern writers spoke of slavery no longer as an evil but in positive terms.

George Fitzhugh in Defense of Slavery

We provide for each slave, in old age and in infancy, in sickness and in health, not according to his labor, but according to his wants. The master's wants are more costly and refined, and he therefore gets a larger share of the profits. A Southern farm is...a joint concern, in which the slave consumes more than the master, of the coarse products, and is far happier, because although the concern may fail, he is always sure of a support; he is only transferred to another master to participate in the profits of another concern; he marries when he pleases, because he knows he will have to work no more with a family than without one, and whether he live or die, that family will be taken care of; he exhibits all the pride of ownership, despises a partner in a smaller concern, "a poor man's negro," boasts of "our crops, horses, fields and cattle"; and is as happy as a human being can be. And why should he not?—He enjoys as much of the fruits of the farm as he is capable of doing, and the wealthiest can do no more.

From: *Sociology for the South* by George Fitzhugh (Richmond, Virginia: A. Morris, 1854).

During the Illinois senatorial race of 1858, Abraham Lincoln debated Stephen A. Douglas on a number of issues surrounding slavery (*North Wind Picture Archives*).

The Expansion of Slavery

The 1858 race for the U.S. Senate seat from Illinois pitted two giants of American history against each other: Abraham Lincoln (1809–1865), a successful Republican lawyer, and Stephen A. Douglas (1813–1861), a Democrat, who had been serving in the Senate since 1847.

Lincoln was the outspoken opponent of the expansion of slavery into the western territories. Douglas, as one of the sponsors of the Kansas-Nebraska Act, was a defender of the right of settlers to bring their slaves with them as they moved West.

The Senate campaign in Illinois in 1858 was one of the most exciting political events in U.S. history. Lincoln and Douglas agreed to debate their positions in front of audiences around the state. Beginning on August 21 at Ottawa, Illinois, and ending with the seventh debate at Alton, Illinois, on October 15, Lincoln and Douglas presented a thorough discussion of the many issues involving slavery. The following statements are from the last debate, in which Lincoln and Douglas argue whether or not the Declaration of Independence applies to all people or to whites only. (Audience reactions are included in brackets.)

Seventh Lincoln-Douglas Debate: Douglas's Speech

But the Abolition party really thinks that under the Declaration of Independence the negro is equal to the white man, and that negro equality is an inalienable right conferred by the Almighty, and hence, that all human laws in violation of it are null and void. With such men it is no use for me to argue. I hope that the signers of the Declaration of Independence had no reference to negroes at all when they declared all men to be created equal. They did not mean negro, nor the savage Indians, nor the Fejee Islanders, nor any other barbarous race. They were speaking of white men. ["It's so," "it's so," and cheers.] They alluded to men of European birth and European descent—to white men, and to none others, when they declared that doctrine. ["That's the truth."] I hold that this government was established on the white basis. It was established by white men for the benefit of white men and their posterity forever, and should be administered by white men, and none others. But it does not follow, by any means, that merely because the negro is not a citizen, and merely because he is not our equal, that, therefore, he should be a slave. On the contrary, it does follow, that we ought to extend to the negro race, and to all other dependent races all the rights, all the privileges, and all the immunities which they can exercise consistently with the safety of society. Humanity requires that we should give them all these privileges; christianity commands that we should extend those privileges to them. The question then arises what are those privileges, and what is the nature and extent of them. My answer is that that is a question which each State must answer for itself.

○ ○ ○

Seventh Lincoln-Douglas Debate: Lincoln's Reply

At Galesburg the other day, I said in answer to Judge Douglas, that three years ago there never had been a man, so far as I knew or believed, in the whole world, who had said that the Declaration of Independence did not include negroes in the term "all men." I re-assert it to-day. I assert that Judge Douglas and all his friends may search the whole records of the country, and it will be a matter of great astonishment to me if they shall be able to find that one human being three years ago had ever uttered the astounding sentiment that the term "all men" in the Declaration did not include the negro. Do not let me be misunderstood. I know that more than three years ago there were men who, finding this assertion constantly in the way of their schemes to bring about the ascendancy and perpetuation of slavery, *denied the truth of it.* I know that Mr. Calhoun and all the politicians of his school denied the truth of the Declaration. I know that it ran along in the mouths of some Southern men for a period of years, ending at last in that shameful though rather forcible declaration of Pettit of Indiana, upon the floor of the United States Senate, that the Declaration of Independence was in that respect "a self-evident lie," rather than a self-evident truth. But I say, with a perfect knowledge of all this hawking at the Declaration without directly attacking it, that three years ago there never had lived a man who had ventured to assail it in the sneaking way of pretending to believe it and then asserting it did not include the negro. [Cheers.] I believe the first man who ever said it was Chief Justice Taney in the Dred Scott case, and the next to him was our friend Stephen A. Douglas. [Cheers and laughter.] And now it has become the catch-word of the entire party. I would like to call upon his friends everywhere to consider how they have come in so short a time to view this matter in a way so entirely different from their former belief to ask whether they are not being borne along by an irresistible current— whither, they know not. [Great applause.]

From: *Abraham Lincoln: Speeches and Writings, 1832–1858* (New York: The Library of America, 1989). Courtesy of The Library of America.

Frederick Douglass
(*Library of Congress*).

Emotions of a Slave

Frederick Douglass, a renowned abolitionist, believed that the emancipation of the slaves was only the beginning of their struggles. He was a major figure who played a leading role in mobilizing African Americans in the 1800s in their quest for freedom and equality.

Born in Maryland in about 1817, Douglass was the son of an African-American female slave and a white father. After escaping from slavery in 1838, he adopted

The title page of a published song dedicated to Frederick Douglass by another abolitionist. Lithograph by E. W. Bouvé (*Library of Congress*).

the last name *Douglass* and settled in Massachusetts, were he worked as a laborer. In 1841, he joined the Massachusetts Anti-Slavery Society and became one of its most skillful and popular speakers.

Douglass, who had learned to read and write while still a slave, published his *Narrative of the Life of Frederick Douglass* in 1845. Fearing that the publication of this book—passages from which follow—would lead to his capture as a runaway slave, he fled to England. He did not return to the United States until 1847, when English friends purchased his freedom. Douglass then settled in Rochester, New York, where he founded an abolitionist newspaper, the *North Star*.

When the Civil War started, Douglass organized two regiments of African Americans from Massachusetts to fight on the Union side. During this time, he became a friend of Abraham Lincoln and was often called to the White House to advise the president. In later life, he was marshal of the District of Columbia and U.S. minister to Haiti. He died February 20, 1895, after attending a women's suffrage meeting.

Youth as a Slave

I was born in Tuckahoe, near Hillsborough, and about twelve miles from Easton, in Talbot county, Maryland. I have no accurate knowledge of my age, never having seen any authentic record containing it. By far the larger part of the slaves know as little of their ages as horses know of theirs, and it is the wish of most masters within my knowledge to keep their slaves thus ignorant. I do not remember to have ever met a slave who could tell of his birthday.

They seldom come nearer to it than planting-time, harvest-time, cherry-time, spring-time, or fall-time. A want of information concerning my own was a source of unhappiness to me even during childhood. The white children could tell their ages. I could not tell why I ought to be deprived of the same privilege. I was not allowed to make any inquiries of my master concerning it. He deemed all such inquiries on the part of a slave improper and impertinent, and evidence of a restless spirit. The nearest estimate I can give makes me now between twenty-seven and twenty-eight years of age. I came to this, from hearing my master say, some time during 1835, I was about seventeen years old....

I have often been utterly astonished, since I came to the north, to find persons who could speak of the singing, among slaves, as evidence of their contentment and happiness. It is impossible to conceive of a greater mistake. Slaves sing most when they are most unhappy. The songs of the slave represent the sorrows of his heart; and he is relieved by them, only as an aching heart is relieved by its tears. At least, such is my experience. I have often sung to drown my sorrow, but seldom to express my happiness. Crying for joy, and singing for joy, were alike uncommon to me while in the jaws of slavery. The singing of a man cast away upon a desolate island might be as appropriately considered as evidence of contentment and happiness, as the singing of a slave; the songs of the one and of the other are prompted by the same emotion.

From: *Narrative of the Life of Frederick Douglass, An American Slave* by Frederick Douglass (Boston: Anti-Slavery Office, 1845).

Abolition

John Brown was a white abolitionist who led an unsuccessful attack at Harpers Ferry, Virginia, in 1859. He was born on May 9, 1800, in Torrington, Connecticut, and grew up in Ohio. Before becoming a passionate abolitionist, he ran a number of failed businesses.

In 1855, he and five of his sons migrated to the Kansas Territory to help win the future state for the antislavery cause. The following year, he and a small group of men, including four of his sons, killed five proslavery men. This gained him national attention and was reported in the abolitionist press.

In 1859, Brown and a group of his followers rented a farm near Harpers Ferry, Virginia, and began planning an armed revolt that they hoped would free all slaves. Their plan was to establish a free area in the mountains to which slaves could flee. On the night of October 16, 1859, Brown and 22 followers attacked and captured a U.S. Army arsenal in Harpers Ferry. Within two days, however, the band was defeated and captured by U.S. Marines led by Colonel Robert E. Lee (1807–1870), later the head of the Confederate army.

John Brown was tried and was then executed on December 2, 1859. A passage from his trial follows. His rebellion shocked the South and helped push the country further toward civil war. In the North, many abolitionists proclaimed Brown a hero. His dignity and courage during his trial and execution helped him win sympathy as a martyr among some people.

A small slave child is blessed by John Brown before his execution in 1859. Brown led the raid on Harpers Ferry, which rallied the abolitionist movement (*Library of Congress*).

John Brown Addresses the Court at His Trial, 1859

I did not ask for any quarter at the time I was taken. I did not ask to have my life spared. The Governor of the State of Virginia tendered me his assurance that I should have a fair trial; and under no circumstances whatever, will I be able to have a fair trial. If you seek my blood, you can have it at any moment, without this mockery of a trial. I have had no counsel. I have not been able to advise with any one. I know nothing about the feelings of my fellow-prisoners, and am utterly unable to attend in any way to my own defence. My memory don't serve me. My health is insufficient, although improving. There are mitigating circumstances that I would urge in our favor, if a fair trial is to be allowed us. But if we are to be forced with a mere form—a trial for execution—you might spare yourselves that trouble. I am ready for my fate. I do not ask a trial. I beg for no mockery of a trial—no insult—nothing but that which conscience gives, or cowardice would drive you to practise. I ask again to be excused from the mockery of a trial. I do not even know what the special design of this examination is. I do not know what is to be the benefit of it to the Commonwealth. I have now little further to ask, other than that I may not be foolishly insulted, only as cowardly barbarians insult those who fall into their power.

From: *The Life, Trial, and Execution of Captain John Brown* (New York: Robert DeWitt, 1859). Reprinted in © 1969 by Mnemosyne Publishing Co.

CHAPTER 3

IN THE MIDST OF WAR

The Battle Begins

The Confederacy—officially the Confederate States of America—was the name of the 11 Southern states whose secession (withdrawal) from the Union during 1860 and 1861 led to the outbreak of the Civil War on April 12, 1861. When the war began, few people in the North or South thought it would last very long. Even the first large-scale military action, the Confederate bombardment of Fort Sumter, had resulted in only one casualty—a dead Union mule.

It was not surprising then, that when word reached Washington in July 1861 that Union military forces were moving against a Confederate position in northern Virginia, many curiosity seekers put their picnic baskets in their horse-drawn carriages and headed south in hopes of seeing a skirmish. What they saw instead was an unexpectedly bloody fight—the First Battle of Bull Run—that resulted in thousands of wounded or dead soldiers.

By the end of 1861, hope had faded for an early end to the war, which continued until April 1865. By the end of the war, more than 620,000 men had died—360,000 Union soldiers and 260,000 Confederates. More than half had died of diseases—tuberculosis, diphtheria—and infections from wounds. The rest were killed in battle. America had seen more casualties during this war than in all of its other wars combined.

It is safe to say that no one in the United States—Northerner or Southerner—was unaffected by the Civil War. As the war dragged on, battles became more and more bloody. One of those battles, the greatest battle ever fought in the Western Hemisphere, took place at Gettysburg, Pennsylvania, from July 1 to July 3, 1863. General Robert E. Lee's Confederate forces were trying to invade the North, but they met a large Union army

The Battle of Gettysburg was one of the most important victories for the North. Fought in July 1863, the battle cost the South about 20,000 men. This lithograph is by Currier and Ives (*North Wind Picture Archives*).

Union general William Tecumseh Sherman, photographed by Mathew Brady in 1865 (*National Archives*).

Confederate general Robert E. Lee (*Library of Congress*).

under General George Meade (1815–1872) in southern Pennsylvania. When the battle was finished, more than 50,000 troops lay dead or wounded, and the Confederacy's hopes for military victory were ended.

The war continued for another year and a half after Gettysburg. In the fall of 1864, Union general William Tecumseh Sherman (1820–1891) marched an army of 60,000 from Atlanta to Savannah, Georgia, freeing slaves and burning and plundering everything in their path, including civilian property.

Throughout the war, soldiers on both sides tried to keep in touch with home by writing letters. The letter that follows was written by Union private Amos Steere. The Union soldier was with the 25th Massachusetts Volunteer Infantry, serving as a member of the regimental band and also as a stretcher bearer. In this letter to his sister, Steere describes what it feels like to be in the midst of a ferocious battle.

A Union Soldier Writes Home

New Bern, N.C.
May 2nd, 1862

DEAR SISTER LUCY:

In one of your letters written to me I believe you wrote asking of me to give you some information in regard to a person's feeling when upon the battle-field. I can only speak for one, but have heard the remarks of a great number and their feelings are as different as their minds are at home or upon any subject.

As for my own, when we were marching along (on our march up the river road to New Bern) the next morning (after encamping out all night in the rain without any covering) up the road in front of the enemy's works, I was startled by the sound of a cannon directly ahead of us, the Regt. [regiment] having just turned in to the right along the woods, we being in the rear of the Regt. They had just got past the turn of the road, which left us in front, then the 27th [regiment], being the next in advance.

The instant I heard the report, whiz and spat came the ball. It struck in the road about ten feet from me, spattering the mud into some of the boys' faces. At that time I thought it best to get out of the range of that gun and acted accordingly. I crossed the road into an open field, with two or three build-ings upon it. There we established our hospital, or at least were to do so, but before we had got half-way across, the fire had begun to be terrible. I did not expect to get to the buildings without being hit, but fortunately there was not one of us hurt through the engagement.

After crossing the field and arriving at those houses, we found we were in more danger than before, for we were directly in front of their field pieces. The distance was short of a half mile and only but a trifle farther from their water battery—of which four of their heavy guns could be brought to bear upon us. I believe there was only three or four shots fired from that battery, as they were waiting to get a larger haul but was whipped before they were aware of it. As I said before, when we were at those houses the cannon balls, shells and bullets in abundance were flying all around us.

To add to our misery, one of our gun boats opened fire, intending to throw the shells over in amongst us. One burst in the ground just seven rods from where we stood. The next burst over the house. Then we thought best to make our quarters

A young Confederate soldier lies dead. This photograph was taken by Thomas C. Roche (*Library of Congress*).

somewhere else, so we did, but how we got out of it without one of us being wounded is a mystery to me.

I felt the need of religion then if I ever did, and wished that I might be a Christian so that I shall in time of battle and at all other times be prepared to meet my God in peace. I have met with no change of heart as yet, but long for the time to come when it will be as easy for me to do right as it is for me to do wrong. Others say that they had not the least feelings of fear from the beginning and others say that they began to think they were cowards, and others something else.

I think as a general thing those at home that are naturally timid are the ones here that have the least fear. For a sample, I will give Patrick Cronan, Co. E, 25th Mass. [regiment]. He was a sort of street bully as they term it at home and has fought one prize fight here at New Bern. He skulked out of the fight and afterwards was court marshaled and sentenced to wear at guard mounting and through the day a wide board on the back with the word *coward* in capital letters marked on it for five days, then to have his head shaved, the buttons cut from his coat and drummed out of the service. All of that was executed.

Others that it was thought would not fight at all fought the best....

I have no particular news to write except our Fort is nearly completed just outside of the city, of which I will give you a plan. Give my love to Mary if you see her, and all the rest of my friends.

From your brother,
AMOS STEERE

From: U.S. Military History Institute Archives; Lewis Leigh Collection. Reprinted by permission of Mr. Lewis Leigh, Jr.

African-American soldiers were a valuable force in the fight against the Confederacy. Here, recruits march up Beekman Street in New York City after enlisting for the North (*Library of Congress*).

Prejudice in the Military

The Civil War was a great turning point in American history for both white people and African Americans. Slavery was destroyed forever, and the country, despite its wounds, emerged as a powerful, industrialized nation that was prepared to assume its place as a world leader. During this bloody conflict, African Americans played a crucial role in liberating themselves from slavery. Until recent times, their story went largely untold in the history books that traditionally have been written by white men. Today, however, we know not only about the influence of great African-American leaders like Frederick Douglass, but also of the commitment and courage of hundreds of thousands of ordinary African Americans.

At the beginning of the war, African Americans were not allowed to serve as soldiers in the Union army, even though those in the North who were free continually petitioned President Lincoln to let them bear arms. Frederick Douglass also urged Lincoln to admit African Americans into the army.

After early Union military defeats, Lincoln came to realize that African Americans were a valuable resource in the struggle against the Confederacy. The very sight of African-American soldiers, Lincoln once said, would strike fear in the hearts of white Southerners. Once African Americans were officially allowed to serve, they volunteered in great numbers. By the end of the war, more than 100,000 African-American men were in the Union forces—making up about one tenth of the entire army.

Despite their courage in battle, African-American soldiers faced enormous prejudice. They were not allowed to serve in regiments with white soldiers, but the leaders of their regiments had to be white. In addition, they were often paid less for the same service performed by white soldiers. Lincoln was opposed to any double standard, insisting that African Americans receive the same pay as whites. In the following letter, an African-American soldier named James Henry Gooding writes an eloquent and moving plea to President Lincoln for equal pay.

An African-American Soldier Writes to President Lincoln

Morris Island, S.C.
September 28, 1863

YOUR EXCELLENCY ABRAHAM LINCOLN:

Your Excellency will pardon the presumption of an humble individual like myself, in addressing you, but the earnest solicitation of my comrades in arms besides the genuine interest felt by myself in the matter is my excuse, for placing before the Executive head of the Nation our Common Grievance.

On the 6th of the last Month, the Paymaster of the Department informed us, that if we would decide to receive the sum of $10 (ten dollars) per month, he would come and pay us that sum, but that, on the sitting of Congress, the Regt. [regiment] would, in his opinion, be allowed the other 3 (three).* He did not give us any guarantee that this would be, as he hoped; certainly he had no authority for making any such guarantee, and we cannot suppose him acting in any way interested.

Now the main question is, are we Soldiers, or are we Laborers? We are fully armed, and equipped, have done all the various duties pertaining to a Soldier's life, have conducted ourselves to the complete satisfaction of General Officers, who were, if anything, prejudiced against us, but who now accord us all the encouragement and honors due us; have shared the perils and labor of reducing the first strong-hold that flaunted a Traitor Flag; and more, Mr. President, to-day the Anglo-Saxon

* **Editor's note:** White soldiers were paid $13 per month, while the black soldiers were paid only $10.

Mother, Wife, or Sister are not alone in tears for departed Sons, Husbands and Brothers. The patient, trusting descendant of Afric's Clime have dyed the ground with blood, in defence of the Union, and Democracy. Men, too, your Excellency, who know in a measure the cruelties of the iron heel of oppression, which in years gone by, the very power their blood is now being spilled to maintain, ever ground them in the dust.

But when the war trumpet sounded o'er the land, when men knew not the Friend from the Traitor, the Black man laid his life at the altar of the Nation,—and he was refused. When the arms of the Union were beaten, in the first year of the war, and the Executive called for more food for its ravenous maw, again the black man begged the privilege of aiding his country in her need, to be again refused.

And now he is in the War, and how has he conducted himself? Let their dusky forms rise up, out of the mires of James Island,* and give the answer. Let the rich mould around Wagner's* parapets be upturned, and there will be found an eloquent answer. Obedient and patient and solid as a wall are they. All we lack is a paler hue and a better acquaintance with the alphabet.

Now your Excellency, we have done a Soldier's duty. Why can't we have a Soldier's pay?

JAMES HENRY GOODING

* **Editor's note:** James Island and Fort Wagner were both sites of battles where large numbers of African-American soldiers died and were buried.

From: *A Documentary History of the Negro People in the United States,* Herbert Aptheker, ed. (New York: Citadel Press, 1951). Copyright © 1969 by Herbert Aptheker. Published in arrangement with Carol Publishing Group.

Abraham Lincoln
(*Library of Congress*).

Lincoln: A Voice for Democracy

Abraham Lincoln is considered by many historians to have been the greatest American president. He led his country to victory in a bloody civil war, oversaw the destruction of slavery, and gave voice to many of the ideas that still guide our democratic government. He expressed these ideas in a number of speeches, which today remain among the most enduring documents of American history. Selections from two of these documents follow.

On March 4, 1865, Lincoln, upon taking the presidential oath for the second time, pondered the fate of the American people. He suggested that perhaps the war, which would end the following month, had been God's punishment for all Americans for the sin of slavery, and he called for unity and forgiveness.

In his Emancipation Proclamation, a military measure which was issued in a preliminary version on September 22, 1862, and which went into effect on January 1, 1863, Lincoln's aim was to weaken the strength of the Confederacy. Under its terms, slaves were freed only in those portions of the country still in rebellion. Slaves within the territory of the Union remained slaves. However, the Emancipation Proclamation set in motion the forces that were to lead to the eventual abolition of all slavery in the United States in 1865 with the passage of the Thirteenth Amendment to the U.S. Constitution.

Second Inaugural Address

Fondly do we hope—fervently do we pray—that this mighty scourge of war may speedily pass away. Yet, if God wills that it continue, until all the wealth piled by the bond-man's two hundred and fifty years of unrequited toil shall be sunk, and until every drop of blood drawn with the lash, shall be paid by another drawn with the sword, as was said three thousand years ago, so still it must be said "the judgments of the Lord, are true and righteous altogether."

With malice toward none; with charity for all; with firmness in the right, as God gives us to see the right, let us strive on to finish the work we are in; to bind up the nation's wounds; to care for him who shall have borne the battle, and for his widow, and his orphan—to do all which may achieve and cherish a just, and a lasting peace, among ourselves, and with all nations.

March 4, 1865

From: *The World's Great Speeches*, Lewis Copeland and Lawrence W. Lamm, eds. (New York: Dover, 1958).

Perhaps Lincoln's most famous words are in the Gettysburg Address, delivered on November 19, 1863, at the dedication of the military cemetery near the site of the great battle a few months earlier. The Gettysburg Address was Lincoln's way of applying the principles of the Declaration of Independence to the Constitution. For Lincoln, the Declaration of Independence was the founding document of the country. The Constitution was more of a vehicle of government, and because it had permitted slavery to exist, it was flawed and needed to be amended.

Address delivered at the dedication of the cemetery at Gettysburg.

Four score and seven years ago our fathers brought forth on this continent, a new nation, conceived in Liberty, and dedicated to the proposition that all men are created equal.

Now we are engaged in a great civil war, testing whether that nation, or any nation so conceived and so dedicated, can long endure. We are met on a great battle-field of that war. We have come to dedicate a portion of that field, as a final resting place for those who here gave their lives, that that nation might live. It is altogether fitting and proper that we should do this.

But, in a larger sense, we can not dedicate— we can not consecrate— we can not hallow— this ground. The brave men, living and dead, who struggled here, have consecrated it, far above our poor power to add

or detract. The world will little note, nor long remember what we say here, but it can never forget what they did here. It is for us the living, rather, to be dedicated here to the unfinished work which they who fought here have thus far so nobly advanced. It is rather for us to be here dedicated to the great task remaining before us— that from these honored dead we take increased devotion to that cause for which they gave the last full measure of devotion— that we here highly resolve that these dead shall not have died in vain— that this nation, under God, shall have a new birth of freedom— and that government of the people, by the people, for the people, shall not perish from the earth.

Abraham Lincoln

November 19, 1863.

Address at Gettysburg, Pennsylvania

Four score and seven years ago our fathers brought forth on this continent, a new nation, conceived in Liberty, and dedicated to the proposition that all men are created equal.

Now we are engaged in a great civil war, testing whether that nation, or any nation so conceived and so dedicated, can long endure. We are met on a great battle-field of that war. We have come to dedicate a portion of that field, as a final resting place for those who here gave their lives that that nation might live. It is altogether fitting and proper that we should do this.

But, in a larger sense, we can not dedicate—we can not consecrate—we can not hallow—this ground. The brave men, living and dead, who struggled here, have consecrated it, far above our poor power to add or detract. The world will little note, nor long remember what we say here, but it can never forget what they did here. It is for us the living, rather, to be dedicated here to the unfinished work which they who fought here have thus far so nobly advanced. It is rather for us to be here dedicated to the great task remaining before us—that from these honored dead we take increased devotion to that cause for which they gave the last full measure of devotion—that we here highly resolve that these dead shall not have died in vain—that this nation, under God, shall have a new birth of freedom—and that government of the people, by the people, for the people, shall not perish from the earth.

November 19, 1863.

From: *The World's Great Speeches*, Lewis Copeland and Lawrence W. Lamm, eds. (New York: Dover, 1958).

Prisoner-of-War Camps

During the Civil War, thousands of troops on both sides of the long and bloody conflict were captured and held as prisoners. One particularly notorious Confederate prisoner-of-war camp was at Andersonville, Georgia, where conditions were unbelievably brutal and inhumane. While thousands of Confederate soldiers also died of disease because of bad conditions in Union camps in the North, Andersonville has lived on in memory as one of the worst examples of the poor treatment of prisoners.

By the end of the war, more than 12,000 Union soldiers had died in Andersonville, most after contracting any number of infectious diseases, after suffering from severe hunger, and from exposure to the elements. There were few buildings in Andersonville, so most prisoners lived in the open, subject to rain, cold weather, and heat, with blankets as their only protection. There were no sewers, and diseases spread quickly. In addition, food was scarce. Most people who survived looked like living skeletons when they were released.

In the following passage, one of the survivors of Andersonville describes his memories of the deadly conditions under which the Union soldiers lived every day. Today, Andersonville is a National Historic Site that is visited by thousands of people each year.

Andersonville

Inside the camp death stalked on every hand. Death at the hand of the guards, though murder in cold blood, was merciful beside the systematic, studied, absolute murder inside, by slow death, inch by inch!...one-third of the original enclosure was swampy—a mud of liquid filth, voidings from the thousands, seething with maggots in full activity. This daily increased by the necessities of the inmates, being the only place accessible for the purpose. Through this mass of pollution passed the only water that found its way through the Bull Pen. [The water] came to us between the two sources of pollution, the Confederate camp and the cook house; first, the seepage of sinks; second, the dirt and filth emptied by the cook house; then was our turn to use it. I have known over three thousand men to wait in line to get water, and the line was added to as fast as reduced, from daylight to dark, yes, even into the night; men taking turns of duty with men of their mess, in order to hold their place in line, as no one man could stand it alone, even if in the "pink" of physical condition; the heat of the sun, blistering him, or the drenching rains soaking him, not a breath of fresh air, and we had no covering but Heaven's canopy. The air was loaded with unbearable, fever-laden stench from that poison sink of putrid mud and water, continually in motion by the activity of the germs of death. We could not get away from the stink—we ate it, drank it and slept in it (when exhaustion compelled sleep).

From: "Hell and the Survivor: A Civil War Memoir" by C. F. Hopkins, *American Heritage*, Vol. 33, No. 6 (October/November 1982), pp. 78–93. Copyright © 1982. Reprinted by permission of American Heritage, a division of Forbes, Incorporated.

CHAPTER 4

REBUILDING THE NATION

Securing the People's Rights

After the Civil War, the job of putting a fractured nation back together became the main task of the federal government. This enormous job involved a combination of constitutional, economic, and social issues.

Slavery, the major issue over which the Civil War had been fought, was abolished in 1865 by the passage of the Thirteenth Amendment to the Constitution (see page 53). But despite its passage, many problems remained to be debated and solved, most notably those concerning the rights and status of African Americans. On this topic, the North and the South still held widely different views.

Amendment XIII

SECTION 1. Neither slavery nor involuntary servitude, except as a punishment for crime whereof the party shall have been duly convicted, shall exist within the United States, or any place subject to their jurisdiction.

SECTION 2. Congress shall have power to enforce this article by appropriate legislation.

During the turbulent and troubled years that characterized Reconstruction (rebuilding after the Civil War, 1865–1877), white leaders of the former Confederacy were strongly opposed to giving any kind of power to ex-slaves. Even though almost all the states that had seceded were required to ratify (approve) the Thirteenth Amendment in order to be readmitted to the Union, white politicians were still able to find ways to prevent African Americans from exercising the rights they had been given as free citizens.

The Black Codes, a series of laws enacted in various Southern states in 1865–1866, were one way that powerful whites were able to limit the freedoms of African Americans. Under the Black Codes, though former slaves were allowed to marry and own personal property, they were segregated (kept separate) in public places and were forbidden to own valuable property and to testify or sue in courts.

The Republicans were most eager to have African Americans as voters, believing they would support the party of Lincoln, the Great Emancipator. In 1866, the Republican-dominated Congress broadened the powers of the Freedmen's Bureau, an agency designed to protect the rights of former slaves.

AN ORDINANCE ABOLISHING SLAVERY IN MISSOURI

Be it ordained by the people of the State of Missouri in Convention assembled

That hereafter in this State there shall be neither slavery nor involuntary servitude except in punishment of crime whereof the party shall have been duly convicted and all persons held to service or labor as slaves are hereby

DECLARED FREE

By 1865, some gains had been made by blacks in the South, and slavery was outlawed in many states—as this official document shows (*Library of Congress*).

Although the Freedmen's Bureau performed many valuable social and educational tasks in the three years of its existence, as indicated in the description on page 55 of the Freedmen's Bureau courts, it soon became a political organization intent on guaranteeing Republican rule in the South. Politicians from the North, many of whom were employed in the Freedmen's Bureau, threw their belongings into carpetbags and headed for the South, where they were elected to political office with the votes of African Americans. White Southerners detested these so-called carpetbaggers and the Freedmen's Bureau and did everything to prevent the bureau from succeeding.

The Freedmen's Bureau Courts

The freedmen's court is no respecter of persons. The proudest aristocrat and the humblest Negro stand at its bar on an equal footing....

A great variety of business is brought before the Bureau. Here is a Negro-man who has printed a reward offering fifty dollars for information to assist him in finding his wife and children, sold away from him in times of slavery: a small sum for such an object, you may say, but it is all he has, and he has come to the Bureau for assistance.... Yonder is a white woman, who has been warned by the police that she must not live with her husband because he is black, and who has come to claim protection in her marriage relation, bringing proof that she is really a colored woman.... Yonder comes an old farmer with a stout colored boy, to get the Bureau's sanction to a contract they wish to make. "Pull off your hat, Bob," says the old man; "you was raised to that"; for he was formerly the lad's owner.... He is very grateful for what the officers do for him, and especially for the good advice they give the boy....

As they go out, in comes a powerful, short-limbed black in tattered overcoat.... He has made a crop; found everything—mules, feed, implements; hired his own help,—fifteen men and women; managed everything; by agreement he was able to have one half; but, owing to an attempt to swindle him, he has had the cotton attached and now it is not on his account he has come, but he is owing his men wages, and they want something for Christmas, which he thinks reasonable, and he desires the Bureau's assistance to raise three hundred dollars....

Here is a boy, who was formerly a slave, to whom his father, a free man, willed a sum of money, which the boy's owner borrowed, giving his note for it, but never repaid,—for did not the boy and all that he had belong to his master? The worn and soiled bit of paper is produced; and now the owner will have that money to restore, with interest. Lucky for the boy that he kept that torn and dirty scrap carefully hidden all these years!

From: *The South* by J. T. Trowbridge (Hartford, Connecticut: L. Stebbins, 1866).

The Freedmen's Bureau was mostly out of existence in 1869, and during the 1870s, the fate of African Americans in the South was still in the hands of the ruling white classes. Through organized scare tactics, violence, and the imposition of literacy tests, poll taxes, and educational and property requirements, ex-slaves were kept from voting, despite the fact that the right to vote had been guaranteed them in 1870 by the Fifteenth Amendment (below). For the next 95 years, Congress took no action to enforce the Constitution and protect the rights of African Americans.

Amendment XV

SECTION 1. The right of citizens of the United States to vote shall not be denied or abridged by the United States or by any State on account of race, color, or previous condition of servitude.

SECTION 2. The Congress shall have power to enforce this article by appropriate legislation.

In 1965, Congress finally passed the Voting Rights Act, which effectively gave African Americans the right to vote throughout the South for the first time since Reconstruction.

"The First Vote," which appeared in *Harper's Weekly* in 1867 (*Library of Congress*).

The Reality of Freedom

On April 3, 1865, Abraham Lincoln paid a surprise visit to Richmond, Virginia, the capital of the recently defeated Confederacy. As he strolled through the war-torn city, he was quickly recognized and mobbed by former slaves. Some fell to their knees and worshiped the president as if he were a god. In the immediate aftermath of the war, African Americans across the South believed that "Jubilee," the long-awaited freedom, had finally come. "Everybody went wild," said one ex-slave when interviewed years later (see the first excerpt that follows), and "we was...feeling kind of happy-like," commented another former slave. These joyful reactions to freedom were recorded in the book *Lay My Burden Down* (see the second selection).

Proud but Not Rich

Everybody went wild. We felt like heroes, and nobody had made us that way but ourselves. We was free. Just like that, we was free. It didn't seem to make the whites mad, either. They went right on giving us food just the same. Nobody took our homes away, but right off colored folks started on the move. They seemed to want to get closer to freedom, so they'd know what it was—like it was a place or a city. Me and my father stuck, stuck close as a lean tick to a sick kitten. The Gudlows started us out on a range. My father, he'd round up cattle— unbranded cattle—for the whites. They was cattle that they belonged to, all right; they had gone to find water 'long the San Antonio River and the Guadalupe. Then the whites gave me and my father some cattle for our own. My father had his own brand—7B—and we had a herd to start out with of seventy.

We knowed freedom was on us, but we didn't know what was to come with it. We thought we was going to get rich like the white folks. We thought we was going to be richer than the white folks, 'cause we was stronger and knowed how to work, and the whites didn't, and they didn't have us to work for them any more. But it didn't turn out that way. We soon found out that freedom could make folks proud, but it didn't make 'em rich.

From: *Lay My Burden Down,* B. A. Botkin, ed. (Chicago: University of Chicago Press, 1945).

Thankful... and Scared

Lord, Lord, honey! It seems impossible that any of us ever lived to see that day of freedom, but thank God we did.

When Old Master comes down in the cotton patch to tell us 'bout being free, he say, "I hates to tell you, but I knows I's got to—you is free, just as free as me or anybody else what's white." We didn't hardly know what he means. We just sort of huddle round together like scared rabbits, but after we knowed what he mean, didn't many of us go, 'cause we didn't know where to of went. Old Master he say he give us the woods land and half of what we make on it, and we could clear it and work it or starve. Well, we didn't know hardly what to do 'cause he just gives us some old dull hoes and axes to work with; but we all went to work, and as we cut down the trees and the poles he tells us to build the fence round the field and we did, and when we plants the corn and the cotton we just plant all the fence corners full too, and I never seen so much stuff grow in all my born days. Several ears of corn to the stalk, and them big cotton stalks was a-laying over the ground. Some of the old slaves they say they believe the Lord knew something 'bout niggers after all. He lets us put corn in his crib, and then we builds cribs and didn't take long 'fore we could buy some hosses and some mules and some good hogs. Them mangy hogs what our master give us the first year was plumb good hogs after we grease them and scrub them with lye soap. He just give us the ones he thought was sure to die, but he was a-gitting going now, and 'fore long we was a-building better houses and feeling kind of happy-like.

From: *Lay My Burden Down*, B. A. Botkin, ed. (Chicago: University of Chicago Press, 1945).

In the years immediately following the war, it seemed that freedom had indeed arrived. In 1870, African Americans were given the right to vote, and under the protection of the Union Army and the Freedmen's Bureau, many of them had received land and education. Education was a novelty for African-American children, and they were very eager to learn, according to Charlotte Forten, who described her teaching experiences in Georgia in "Life on the Sea Islands."

Education: A Delightful Experience

I never before saw children so eager to learn, although I had had several years' experience in New-England schools. Coming to school is a constant delight and recreation to them. They come here as other children go to play. The older ones, during the summer, work in the fields from early morning until eleven or twelve o'clock, and then come to school, after their hard toil in the hot sun, as bright and as anxious to learn as ever.

...The majority learn with wonderful rapidity. Many of the grown people are desirous of learning to read. It is wonderful how a people who have been so long crushed to the earth...can have so great a desire for knowledge, and such a capacity for attaining it.

From: "Life on the Sea Islands" by Charlotte Forten, *Atlantic Monthly*, Vol. 13 (March 1864), p. 591.

FROM SLAVERY THROUGH RECONSTRUCTION: 1619–1865

1619
The slave trade is introduced into what is now the United States: A Dutch merchant brings 20 Africans to Jamestown, Virginia, to sell.

1831
Nat Turner leads a slave revolt that results in the deaths of 57 white people. Turner is promptly caught and executed.

1839
Theodore Dwight Weld and Angelina Grimké attack the cruelty of slavery in their book, *American Slavery as It Is.*

1852
Harriet Beecher Stowe's *Uncle Tom's Cabin*, a literary classic that criticizes the injustices of slavery, is published.

1858
Abraham Lincoln and Stephen Douglas run against each other in the Illinois senatorial race. Their debates over the issue of slavery become historic.

1859
Hoping to free all slaves, John Brown unsuccessfully attacks the U.S. Army arsenal at Harpers Ferry, Virginia. He is tried and executed.

1860
Abraham Lincoln is elected president of the United States. His party, the Republican Party, is a newly formed coalition of antislavery forces.

1861
The Civil War, a bloody conflict in which the North fights the South, begins. By the end of the war in 1865, more than 620,000 people are dead.

1865
The Thirteenth Amendment to the Constitution is passed by Congress—slavery is abolished and Reconstruction begins.

FOR FURTHER READING

Biel, Timothy. *The Civil War*. San Diego, CA: Lucent Books, 1991.

Chang, Ina. *A Separate Battle: Women and the Civil War*. New York: Lodestar Books, 1991.

Katz, William L. *Breaking the Chains: African-American Slave Resistance*. New York: Atheneum Children's Books, 1990.

Murphy, Jim. *The Boys' War: Confederate and Union Soldiers Talk about the Civil War*. Boston: Clarion Books, 1990.

_____. *The Long Road to Gettysburg*. Boston: Clarion Books, 1992.

Ray, Delia. *Behind the Blue and Gray: The Soldier's Life in the Civil War*. New York: Lodestar Books, 1991.

_____. *A Nation Torn: The Story of How the Civil War Began*. New York: Lodestar Books, 1990.

Reit, Seymour. *Behind Rebel Lines: The Incredible Story of Emma Edmonds, Civil War Spy*. San Diego, CA: Odyssey, 1991.

Stevens, Bryna. *Frank Thompson: Her Civil War Story*. New York: Macmillan Children's Books, 1992.

Wade, Linda R. *Andersonville: A Civil War Tragedy*. Vero Beach, FL: Rourke Enterprises, 1991.

INDEX